Alternative Collects

Prayers to a Disruptive and Compassionate God

— GRAHAM TURNER —

Sacristy Press
PO Box 612, Durham, DH1 9HT

www.sacristy.co.uk

First published in 2018 by Sacristy Press, Durham

Copyright © Graham Turner 2018
The moral rights of the author have been asserted

Sacristy Limited, registered in England & Wales, number 7565667

British Library Cataloguing-in-Publication Data
A catalogue record for the book is available from the British Library

ISBN 978-1-910519-80-6

To David Wightman, who died on 1 January 2018.
He was a wonderful, witty, and prayerful companion on
the road of life, and will be greatly missed by many.

Preface

Some of us have grown up with the church's weekly collects and have taken them for granted as part of the liturgy. Others have stumbled into them when they joined a congregation that makes use of them. For many, though, our attitude to the weekly (or seasonal) collect can sometimes be ambivalent.

On the one hand, there are collects that stick in our minds because they put into words what we could not express properly ourselves. They result in a change between us and God. Then, on the other hand, there are many that seem to simply pass us by. We cannot disagree with their sentiment, but they do not leave any impression on us or alter our encounter with God. They are too general. There is little in these prayers that we find challenging to verbalize as we might do with some of the Psalms or other more gritty prayers of the Bible.

Still, the collect plays an important part in worship in many Christian denominations. Its purpose is to draw together (to "collect") the various themes and elements of the service as well as to draw the people of the congregation into a deeper solidarity.

These alternative collects seek to overcome some of the predictability and generality of the current prayers. Issues of social justice, as well as spirituality, are incorporated. They are more varied in style and seek to introduce elements of risk, danger, and even threat into our unfolding and developing relationship with God. These, though, are tempered by the hope, fresh imagination, and uncompromising love of God. In prayer we encounter God as both disruptive and compassionate. Each collect is rooted in the firm belief that God acts, and that our lives and our futures depend on this.

The collects in this book cover all the Sundays of the church's year and its Principal Feasts; none are included for the Festivals of the Lectionary. These prayers differ in a number of ways from those traditionally used in most churches:

1. They do not necessarily follow the typical structure of address, acknowledgement, request, aspiration, and plea. Their form is as fluid and varied as prayers found among the Psalms and the prophets. Some of these new collects are more of a reflection of where our lives currently stand with God—others are quite specific in their request. The prayers are designed to be used in the context of corporate worship or personal devotions.

2. Each is based upon a selection of readings from the *Common Worship Lectionary* (even in Ordinary Time) or draw their substance from the particular theme of the season or feast. In this they are more closely related to other aspects of the worship than many of the traditional collects.

3. Some are longer than usual. Depending on what the sermon has been about, these collects could be used at the end of the sermon to draw together its different strands.

These alternative collects are offered as a resource to include in the mix when preparing for worship. They can, of course, be adapted and amended for any particular context. Some may find them profitable to use in their own personal devotions as they may express instincts that they had not previously been able to put into words themselves—see the Postscript (page 104) for more on this.

It is only as the church at prayer that we will make sense of our text (the Bible), our context (the universe), and therefore our creator (God). It is my hope that the collects in this book will help in making a contribution towards this.

Contents

Year A

The First Sunday of Advent

Lord of Advent, Lord of all hopefulness;
  this is the time of your coming,
  this is the season of your arrival.
Give us a defiant hope
  that triumphs over pessimism and cynical attitudes,
  that believes you have come to save your people,
  your world, your creation.
In this moment, light a fire in our hearts
  that will not be quenched until your work is done.
Amen.

The Second Sunday of Advent

Come among us, O Advent God,
  for we are grievously hindered by our despair and disbelief.
We had hoped and we had believed,
  yet our world has become a highway of crookedness
  and our souls have been left crying in the wilderness.
Come and deliver us.
Send a small child to lead us.
Baptize us afresh with your Spirit of wisdom and good counsel.
Come and judge to put wrongs right for the poor
  and so remove our discomfort for having more than our fair share.
Come, fill the earth as the waters cover the sea.
Amen.

The Third Sunday of Advent

O bringer of newness from beyond our wildest dreams,
whose promise of coming we heard
    through courageous people of faith.
Transform the aridity of our lives
    and the selfish indulgence of our world,
      as we are no longer brave enough to change ourselves.
Strengthen weak hands and make firm feeble knees,
    for we are a people who cannot stand alone.
We are like reeds badly shaken by storms unexpected
    yet still seeking to be stewards of your mysteries.
Prepare the way, prepare your people, prepare the church;
that we may boldly announce: "Here is your God!"
Amen.

The Fourth Sunday of Advent

You are the God of disgraced and shamed peoples;
    the one who stands alongside those in desperate and hard places.
You prepared Mary and stood by your servant
    in her desperate and hard place:
    pregnant, misunderstood, and alone.
You spoke through angels and dreamers,
    embraces and encounters,
    and announced to us your presence.
Immanuel, be with us and take away our fear,
    that we may be free to choose what is good
    and stand against all that is evil.
Amen.

Christmas Eve

Make us glad, faithful God, as we stand on the cusp of a new dawn,
    as darkness gives way to light
    and the shadow of death is vanquished by new birth.
Guide us into a deep experience of peace
    that is more than mere quietness;
    there your hand will hold us fast.
Cause us to treasure in our hearts
    the only one thing necessary.
Lead us to see life differently
    and find our place in the world in obedience and lowliness.
Amen.

Christmas Day

Today, we see a great light;
a child has been born, your Son has been given—
    God amongst us.
Today is our day of thanksgiving and celebration
    for you have come to set your people free.
Despite so many warnings we were not ready
    to receive your gift of life.
But you make us ready by your very presence.
You have lit the light of hope within us.
You have come to make us new,
for alone we remain tawdry and worn out.
Thank you, God, for the great gift of this day.
Amen.

The First Sunday of Christmas

Great-hearted, generous God,
you came to us in weakness and vulnerability,
    dependent upon inexperienced parents
    and susceptible to violent politics.
You came to be like us, in order that we might become like you.
By embracing our humanity,
    you made us your sisters and brothers.
Take us into other people's worlds
    so that we may see them as family and kinsfolk,
    also created, loved, and called by you.
Amen.

The Second Sunday of Christmas

O Word,
who accommodated yourself among us,
    we see in you what we have not seen elsewhere:
    grace to the full and truth in all its beauty.
In you we recognize God's face.
In you we encounter God's love.
In you we hear God's voice.
Yet we are both honoured and unsettled
    by your presence.
We like what we see in you,
    but we fear what you will see in us.
Steady our anxious dispositions and make still our distracted lives
    that we may receive the gift long expected, given in love.
Amen.

The Epiphany

By leading outsiders from an alien territory
　　to worship the God-child,
you displayed your glory to exotic princes.
Lead us out of our comfortable worlds
　　of managed control and attenuated risk.
Lead us to see in foreign people and places
　　the light of your life and the hope of your love.
Lead conflicted nations on new and untrodden paths
　　of justice and reconciliation,
　　for the sake of sanity,
　　for the sake of the world,
　　for the sake of Jesus Christ,
　　the infant king born among us.
Amen.

The Baptism of Christ

The First Sunday of Epiphany

O God among us,
　　a bruised reed you will not break,
　　nor will your strength grow faint or diminished.
Baptize us afresh into the ways of Jesus.
When you call, may we respond, "Let it be so."
When you speak, may we hear, "This is my child, the beloved."
As he walked, let us walk obediently.
As he died, let us die daily.
As he rose, let us rise eternally.
Amen.

The Second Sunday of Epiphany

O God, who called us before we even knew ourselves
    and chose us along with many other unlikely people,
make all things new and make us new.
Invite us once again to come and see the life of your Son among us.
We will wait and be patient for your calling and voice of reassurance.
Then we will proclaim, "We have found the Christ":
    the gift and generosity of God.
Amen.

The Third Sunday of Epiphany

O Love uncontainable,
    in all our weakness renew us,
    in all our darkness enlighten us,
    in all our division unite us.
Remind us again of the utter foolishness of your message,
    that the cross of dying has the power to save and bring us life.
Draw us out of the shadows to see that newness has dawned,
    and lift our burdens,
        imposed by other's selfishness and our own stupidity,
that we may keep step with the master, Jesus.
Amen.

The Fourth Sunday of Epiphany

You are God, the dispeller of darkness and unbelief,
    the quencher of thirsty palates,
    the provider of bread to relieve our aching hunger.
In your upside-down, back-to-front world
    our wisdom is mere foolishness
    and our best attempts count for nothing.
But there is nowhere your love does not reach.
It is our priceless refuge,
    our reason to boast and hope,
    and oxygen for our gasping souls.
We do not know whether we are coming or going
    in our busy, activist worlds,
but in your Spirit-filled world we are assured
    that you are only ever coming.
Amen.

The Presentation of Christ in the Temple
Candlemas

O Child, destined for the downfall and rising of many,
    we cautiously present ourselves to you;
you, presented to us for the price of two young birds.
As you became bone of our bones, flesh of our flesh,
    and brother to us all, may we become like you:
    champions of justice,
    ministers of consolation,
    and disturbers of complacency.
You came, not to serve angels but people like us.
And now we will no longer serve the gods
    of our self-centred aspirations, but only you.
Amen.

Proper 1

We have to admit, O God, the message is not complicated,
    but we make it so.
The task is not impossible, but we believe it to be so.
The powers are not all-powerful, but we behave as if they are so.
You, though, are the loosener of the bonds of injustice,
    and you call us to join you.
You are the liberator of oppressed people,
    and you call us to work with you.
You are the feeder of the hungry,
    and you call us to serve alongside you.
There is no need for lofty words or paragraphs of worldly wisdom.
In Christ, and in him crucified,
    is all the demonstration of power we need.
Amen.

Proper 2

Show us your presence, O God,
    in a culture dominated by decadence, adversity, and death.
Show us the weakness of our human inclinations
    manifested in rivalry, mistrust, and fearfulness.
Help us to choose life, not destruction, and to find our
    common purpose begun, continued, and ended in you.
Lead us to live undivided lives,
    where our "Yes" means yes
    and our "No" is exactly what it says.
We wish to prosper
    but only within the economy of your love
    and not at the expense of those less powerful
    or less fortunate than ourselves.
Amen.

Proper 3

Holy God, far, far away and beyond us,
    yet closer to us than our own respiration;
you are the lover of the enemy and friend to every neighbour,
    the hater of injustice and all forms of exploitation.
Incline our ears to hear messages previously unheard.
Turn our eyes to see beauty and goodness
    in people and places previously ignored.
As your Spirit burns passionately within us
    make us holy, not by lofty words and concepts,
        but by acts of compassionate love.
Amen.

The Second Sunday before Lent

Despite what others have told us, Creator God,
    you made us to reflect on earth
    who you have always, ever been.
You created us out of the stuff of stars to be fruitful, good, and rested.
Today we groan and moan and long and labour to become, once again,
    the children of God you always intended us to be.
In moments of sabbath rest, cause us to find again the secrets
    of the lilies of the fields and the birds of the air;
        the place where there is no angst, fretting, or anxious striving.
Only then will we find our precious God-filled humanity.
Amen.

The Sunday next before Lent

We will wait until you change us, O God.
We will wait, even though nations are in uproar
    and many mutter empty threats.
We will wait and not rush in to follow cleverly devised myths.
We will wait for the prophetic message,
    not contrived by human wilfulness.
We will wait while in your presence;
    we will not seek to control the encounter.
We will wait until we know that we too
    are also eternally beloved of you.
Amen.

Ash Wednesday

We have come to repent and return to you, the guardian of our souls.
You have waited and watched for us to come.
Our shame has held us prisoner and our fear has kept us paralysed.
But now we are ready to approach the God
    who hates nothing that he has made.
We were slow to learn that you have not come
    to condemn and annihilate,
and we were reluctant to accept that you look with pity, not blame.
So today may we come to you in humility, not dread.
Amen.

The First Sunday of Lent

O God of empty places,
silence and solitude stalk us
    through these early days of our Lenten journey.
While tempted as you were in Christ,
    we surrender ourselves too easily to distraction,
    and seek out crowded places where we can hide.
So take us to places of quietness and hold us there.
Lead us into the aloneness of our souls.
In the wildernesses of life we know too keenly our weaknesses.
Teach us the lessons that can only be learnt
    in the places we once thought empty and useless,
    but now find to be full of you and your angels.
Amen.

The Second Sunday of Lent

Lord, as Abraham chose the path of greatness,
    so we also want to be great.
And, like Abraham, we do not desire greatness
    as paraded by the world,
    cheaply given and easily taken away.
We only want greatness as you understand such stature
    in your inside-out, bottom-at-the-top, and topsy-turvy world.
We want what will nurture our souls
    and sustain them in our life-sapping, hope-robbing culture.
So bring us to birth again in your Spirit,
    by your Spirit, and of your Spirit.
And in your wind-blowing unpredictability
    take us to what we cannot yet see.
Amen.

The Third Sunday of Lent

O prophet without a bucket, offering life-renewing encounters
    to women of dubious morals and men with little conscience,
by you we are gifted great peace.
Stop us from becoming embittered
    in order that our suffering may mature into endurance.
Keep us from turning resentful
    in order that our endurance
    may produce in us rich character.
And when you transform us into the people
    you would have us be,
    keep us modest and remind us we are not self-made.
Then, your hope will not disappoint
    and we will forever stay with you.
Amen.

The Fourth Sunday of Lent

Sheep-loving, shepherd God of ancient songs and rhymes,
    you take us to places of deep stillness.
O keeper of our souls,
    accompany us through threatening shadows
    and in strange, veiled darknesses.
We have to admit that, when we are hard-pressed,
    our spirits become somewhat fragile and offendable.
Hold us steady.
Keep us from anxious obsessing.
Turn our habitual blindness into the clarity
    of seeing the beauty of truth.
Then surely, merciful goodness will never be shaken loose from us.
Amen.

The Fifth Sunday of Lent
Passiontide begins

O God,
who always breathes resurrection
    while we fear the death that haunts us daily,
    our bones are dried up, and our hope is lost;
    something will surely need to give.
And so we wait for you again, a sabbath for the soul.
Only you know what can be salvaged.
Only you know what can be brought to life.
Only you know what can be made of such lifeless brokenness.
Speak your life into us.
Raise us from our deadness.
Release your freedom-loving life in us, through us, now, for all people.
Amen.

Palm Sunday

In ordinariness and splendour Jesus made his final journey,
    the beginning of his end.
With great excitement, and some trepidation of reprisal,
    the people proclaimed him King David's son.
Teach us, O God, the power of strong humility
    and the strength of non-violent acting
    in the face of arrogant power-brokers.
Use us as counter-cultural symbols
    in a world hell-bent on seeking dominance and control.
Enliven us with a vitality which reflects our confidence
    in your self-giving Son, our liberating Lord.
Amen.

Maundy Thursday

Lord of Passover, you did not flinch when you touched feet,
    washed feet, or sat with feet in your lap.
These symbols of shame were not repugnant to you,
    nor were they defiling.
If you, our Lord and Teacher, can bear such humbling,
then teach us to carry the shame of others
    and help reduce their burden,
for we are not more mighty than anyone we may encounter.
Amen.

Good Friday

My God, my God, how could you have forsaken him so?
Betrayed and rejected, despised and afflicted,
    stricken and crushed, struck down, cut off and poured out,
    acquainted with disability, numbered among the evil doers;
    yet he did not open his mouth.
We are staggered and silenced that in your almightiness
    you yet allowed evil one last throw
through the violent actions of state and religious authorities,
    and people just like us.
Let us feel a small portion of his forsakenness today,
    in order to taste our liberation in two days' time.
Amen.

Easter Eve

Christ has died, and we flounder in your apparent absence.
Everything has stopped and we do not know what to do.
Our inaction unnerves us and makes us feel impotent.
On this day of stopping, of admitting our loss,
    of grieving what will now not be,
do that work in us that can only happen
    when we are powered down and no longer in control.
Bury our illusions, kill our distorted desires,
    put an end to our hair-brain projects
    that we may be ready for you to rise for all tomorrow.
Amen.

Easter Day

We got it wrong, Lord Jesus Christ!
We did not expect you to rise. Alleluia!
Along with Mary, Salome, and Mary, Peter, James, and John,
    we did not believe your foretelling
    when you spoke of resurrection.
Praise God, we got it wrong!
Out with the old patterns of sin and death!
In with the new order where all is made alive!
You have done it through Christ.
You have done it with Christ.
You have done it in Christ.
Alleluia, we got it wrong! Hope springs eternal.
Amen.

The Second Sunday of Easter

We will never understand, O Risen Lord,
    the mystery of your death and resurrection,
    unless we sense it deep within ourselves.
We will never believe that it is impossible
    for Jesus Christ to be held by death,
    unless we learn to die daily ourselves.
Breathe on us your peace-creating and courage-giving Spirit.
Deliver us from the oppressive regimes of sin and death.
Raise us up to a life of freedom
    far beyond our wildest imaginings.
Embrace us in your ongoing, living tradition
    which is imperishable, undefiled, and unfading.
Amen.

The Third Sunday of Easter

We are a people ever searching, with our digital attachments,
    for knowledge and information, for the elixir of life.
We are foolishly fast of mind and slow of heart.
What we need, though, is you, Lord.
All we require is knowledge of your presence among us.
Slow down our minds and warm up our hearts,
that we may encounter your Spirit in meeting the stranger
    and in the breaking of bread.
When we see you, may we meet you;
when we meet you, may you turn our pain into joy
    and our despondency into hope.
Amen.

The Fourth Sunday of Easter

Tenacious Shepherd, whose faithfulness knows no bounds,
we long to hear your name-speaking voice calling us.
More than the rich material rewards of life,
we want to know that we are known, noticed,
    and listened to by you.
We admit that we hesitate, for your abundant life frightens us.
We are not able to domesticate or co-opt your life
    for our private purposes and projects.
So come and destabilize us with your awe
    and unpredictability, for the sake of life and love.
Amen.

The Fifth Sunday of Easter

O Great Stone,
rejected by important and significant people
    and overlooked by those who wield raw power,
we are shamed and sickened by not having the courage
    to be absolute nobodies in the eyes of the world.
O Great Living Stone,
show us the beauty of power fashioned in brokenness
    and the strength of love rooted in suffering,
for we want to see the Father and follow your alternative way,
    which is eternally truth and life.
Amen.

The Sixth Sunday of Easter

We dimly suspect that you are in all things
    and all things are in you,
but we find this hard to believe
    in the habits and routines of secular life.
Instead, we trust our vain search
    for certainties and simplistic answers
that annoyingly evaporate when they seem
    almost within our grasp.
Remove from us our sense of ordered religious purpose
and place into the centre of our being your gift,
    the Spirit of truth.
Then we will be assured that we too are your offspring.
Amen.

Ascension Day

O bridge-builder God,
the One who brings to us the life of God from heaven
and takes the humanity of creation into the Divine,
place into our hearts the love of building bridges
    between alienated peoples,
the desire to reach beyond our fears,
and the courage to abandon our ambivalence
    that leaves us broken from others.
Clothe us with that unusual power,
    sourced from deep within your heart,
and fill us with a joy that makes little or no sense
    in our crazed and demented world.
Amen.

The Seventh Sunday of Easter

Lord, we want to know "When?"
When will you heal the sick?
When will you stop cruel wars?
When will you end our long exile?
When will you return?
When will your kingdom finally, fully come?
But it is not for us to know the times or the seasons.
Humble us. Give us joy.
Cast out our anxiety, and most of all,
    leave us not comfortless.
Only your life-filled love will stop our pestering and worrying
    about our many "When"-filled questions.
Amen.

Pentecost

O promised, pentecostal God of wind and fire
    and energy and love,
you arrive unexpectedly amongst us
    to instigate prophecy, visions, and dreams.
In our managing and manipulating world
    we attempt to make all things one
    by making all things the same.
But you are one, and in your oneness
    you value and cultivate rich difference
    and amazing diversity.
Help us to trust your love of variety and variability,
    and not to become bewildered or fearful
    of your unpredictable ways.
Amen.

Trinity Sunday

Trinity God, you are One, always One, only ever One;
and you are Three, always Three, only ever Three.
We do not need to manipulate you
 to fit our limited mind-sets
 or our preferred doctrinal assumptions,
so deliver us from this sinful, idolatrous urge.
You are beyond us,
beyond our comprehension, pigeon-holing, and stereotyping.
Yet still you invite us to participate
 in all that constitutes your being.
Help us to lean confidently into your Oneness
 that we may experience your Threeness
 and taste your life eternal.
Amen.

Proper 4

O God of endless generations,
you have filled the earth with good things
 and we have filled it with violence and toxicity.
Despite our inability to mend our ways,
 you have remained for us our refuge and our strength.
In our self-inflicted misery you have not left us
 or abandoned us to our fate.
Teach us how to live your radically different way,
 that relies not on force or intimidation,
 but on faithful loving-kindness.
May we not be ashamed of its apparent exposed weakness,
 but find instead its true hidden power to change all things.
Then we will no longer live as fools but rather as the wise.
Amen.

Proper 5

O name-speaking God,
who breaks into our mundane domesticated worlds
    to call us onto new journeys,
give us the determination and gifts we need
    to abandon our ingrained habits
    and travel instead to places yet unknown.
You call into existence things which at present we cannot see.
You enable us to imagine possibilities that still we do not know.
Through us, show that mercy is better than sacrifice.
Through us, demonstrate that you have come
    for the sake of wrong-doers and misfits.
Through us, reveal your ways once promised of old,
    for our sake, for the world's sake, and for your sake.
Amen.

Proper 6

We are a people who laugh at your promises, O God,
    and mock your humble acts of compassion.
We quiz you, asking:
    "How can your futures be possible
    amid corrosive cynicism and pessimism?
How can your lowliness work
    in a world of brutal competing powers?"
So tell us again that it was while we were weak and helpless
    Christ died for the undeserving.
Remind us once more that it was while we meddled in sin
    he died for us.
Then maybe, just maybe, we will see wonder and tender beauty,
    and the promise of new horizons.
Amen.

Proper 7

Lord, you have enticed us with your goodness
    and drawn us with your love.
Even when we were struck down and covered in misery,
    we turned to you for mercy.
Deep in our being we know
    we have been baptized into Christ's death
    and are united with him in his resurrection.
Nothing is unknown to you:
    the hairs on every head are counted,
    each bird in the sky is recognized,
    every grain of sand is numbered.
Lord, you have enticed us with your goodness;
    never let us be seduced by lesser prizes.
Amen.

Proper 8

How long, O Lord, must we as your people
    bear the shame of being defeated and marginalized?
How long, O Lord, must we face crisis upon crisis
    when the many demand we answer the question, "Why?"
How long, O Lord, will you hide your face from us?
Call us again and call us afresh
    that we may have courage
    while in a contrary and uncertain world.
Call us away from a life of blaming and finger-pointing
    to become dispensers of your grace.
Call us once more to be your disciples.
Amen.

Proper 9

O faithful God, we are a conflicted and confused people.
Our own actions are a mystery to us.
We do what we do not want to do, even the very things we hate.
We do not do what we know to be good and true and right.
Does anything good rest within us?
But you have hidden the answers of these imponderables
    from those who think they are clever
    and squandered them on infants.
We are weary of carrying the heavy burdens
    of trying to get everything right.
Take this weight from us.
Change our hearts, for we cannot do it ourselves.
Your load is light, and this is what we will now carry.
Amen.

Proper 10

In a world where some are strong and many are weak,
    help us not to collude in the misuse of power
    by taking advantage of people with less.
We want to live in the economy of God
    where the mighty are tender to the vulnerable;
    the rich serve the poor;
    and those who are full attend to those who are empty.
Challenge us when we benefit from the dark practices
    that take wealth from the powerless
    and provoke you to hostility.
Be a light to us that we may sense and see the way of your Spirit.
Then we shall be peace to all we meet in a world of brokenness.
Amen.

Proper 11

We have issues with how you deal with us, Lord.
We stick with you through thick and thin
    and still you do not bless us.
But we are not going to loosen our grip
    or let our hold on you slip from us,
      for you know us thoroughly and intimately.
We cannot escape you, and we will not let you escape us.
If you need to uproot and discomfort us
    then let it be so.
If you need to expose our waywardness and hypocrisy
    then let it be so.
Only bless us, and bless us richly.
Amen.

Proper 12

We have forgotten and not remembered
    that you, Lord, have kept your covenant with us.
We have not prayed;
    we no longer know how to pray.
Thank goodness you still pray on our behalf,
    with groans and sighs that go beyond
    the superficiality of our words.
You are for us. You are eternally for us.
We are forever connected with you,
    participating in the mystery of your being.
Take what is small and insignificant
    from the earthiness of our lives
    and grow from it something fruitful.
Amen.

Proper 13

We follow you, Lord, in anguish and in sorrow.
We are misunderstood, maltreated, and belittled
    for our faith and trust in you.
Sometimes we flirt with the notion
    of putting all we have in you to one side.
So we need to hear the gospel again.
We need to hear you speak once more.
We need you to feed us with food eternal:
    blessed, broken, and given.
Then we will be filled, and relieved of our angst and our sorrow.
Amen.

Proper 14

Other people think us strange
    when we live amongst them as aliens.
You call us to confess you Lord,
    not for a weird tribal identity,
    nor to stand out and be peculiar,
    but to be heralds of your better way.
Keep us from being seduced
    by the pull of seeking status and security
    outside of your design.
Hold us firm amid the storms of life that loosen our grip on you.
Give us courage to be an incongruous people
    in order that we may be a sign for many.
Keep us well supplied with faith,
    then we will be kept from our fears.
Amen.

Proper 15

Confront us with your outspoken voice, O God.
Address us by means of unlikely people and circumstances.
Make us listen when you speak in unexpected ways:
    through brokenness, through waywardness,
    through the bizarre, through daily ordinariness;
help us to recognize your voice
    amongst the many competing sounds we hear.
And when we hear the uninvited and unwelcomed truth,
    keep us from taking offence.
Instead, open us to your staggering possibilities
    and complacency-destroying gospel.
Amen.

Proper 16

O Son of Man, we live amongst people
    fearful of losing position
    and scared about losing control.
But your word is carried to us
    by children and powerless people:
    unexpected and unnoticed.
When the troubles of life threaten to overwhelm us,
come to our aid in your peculiar way.
When the pressures of life force us to conform,
come, renew our thinking and embolden us, we pray.
For you alone carry the secret of living alternatively
    in a world of dominating powers.
O Son of Man, come to us as we pray.
Amen.

Proper 17

O Lord,
we live in a world of tragic pain and pointless loss.
  The innocent suffer.
  The down-trodden languish.
People of goodwill agonize over the pain of the world.
But who are we, as an inconsequential people,
  to do anything about all of this?
Yet you choose what is despised and lowly
  to defeat and overcome evil.
So help us to love the cruellest of enemies,
  to be patient in testing times,
  and to hold on to what is good.
May our love be genuine and our actions thoughtful and kind.
We do not need great wealth – you are all the riches we need.
Amen.

Proper 18

O Christ,
you instruct us to owe no-one anything except to love,
yet we bear the heavy burden of our insatiable greed
  and our arrogant pretence.
We are heavily indebted to others and we fritter our lives away.
It is time for us to wake up to our present hopelessness
  and lay aside the darkness of our lives.
We will therefore do all we can
  to put right broken and damaged relationships.
We will loosen our attachments
  to people and possessions that have enslaved us.
We will choose to live in freedom and in joy.
Amen.

Proper 19

O God from beyond our horizons,
    there is something about you
    that makes us a frightened people.
Your pillar of cloud and your trembling mountains,
your demands to forgive,
    and your audacious inclusion of seemingly unworthy people
    do not sit easily in our self-ordered worlds.
Take from us the terror of your presence
    that we may live with respect and honour
    for the extensiveness of your being
    throughout the cosmos.
To you, Lord of the living and the dead, we pray.
Amen.

Proper 20

We love to moan and grumble,
    unable to find contentment in all that you have given.
O God, create in us truly grateful hearts
    that appreciate your great provision.
Teach us to search for you
    and seek your face in all things.
Cause us to live in the oneness of the Spirit
    and help us to learn to die while still we live.
Then, in thankfulness and discovery,
    in unity and transformation,
    we will live without envy and in peace.
Amen.

Proper 21

You journey to us, O Christ,
    in order that we may journey with you.
You risked your reputation
    and dared to live among a people immersed in misery.
Help us to follow your example of self-emptying,
    marked by service and joy.
Give us endurance as we travel,
    that the valleys we encounter may not cause us to lose heart
    nor tempt us to settle into bitterness and self-interest.
Mark us with your compassion, strong and tender.
Amen.

Proper 22

You are the Lord our God
    who brought us out from houses of slavery
    and cleansed us from our secret flaws.
You have breathed new life into us.
You have become the rejected one
    as we surely needed a victim.
But your brokenness has become our foundation
    and your resurrection, our only hope.
May we not fear loss,
    so that we may be free from anxiety-driven lives.
Amen.

Proper 23

Because we have been loyal to the rituals of our tradition,
    we wrongly believe we have not turned to other gods.
Because we have signed our religious designation
    to include the name of Christ,
      we wrongly believe we have not bowed to other powers.
Because we regularly sing the hymns and songs
    of the congregation,
      we wrongly believe we have not turned our hearts from you.
But, Lord, we are a stiff-necked people
    who have exchanged glory for a collection of commodities
    and passing reputations.
Urge us to be faithful to you
    as our names are written in your book.
Amen.

Proper 24

Lord, we are ambivalent about who we are,
    sometimes full of self-hatred,
    sometimes full of self-adulation.
But you put it simply and plainly: we are your people.
You address us and call us by name.
We, though, cannot look you in the face
    for fear we could not bear your gaze.
Help us to receive your Word with joy,
    unfiltered by our easy explanations
    of things too deep for us to understand.
Teach us to be wise
    as we live among the violent economies of the world.
Amen.

Proper 25

We only have the stamina to trust in you, O God,
    because we do not have to invent tactics to survive.
As your church, we do not need to stoop to deceit
    or draw on impure motives,
nor do we need to resort to the tricks
    of the corporations or other insecure empires.
You have been our refuge and resource over countless generations.
Your covenant of love has never run dry or been expended.
You do not call us to greed or self-aggrandisement,
    but simply to obey your command
    to love you and our neighbour.
This will be enough for us.
Amen.

All Saints' Day

1st November

From every tribe and language,
from every continent and nation,
from every stratum of society the saints of the Lord are one.
Knitted together, bound together,
    and won together by Christ on the cross.
Come, O Lord, and teach us to live as a people
    who sit and mourn with those who grieve,
    make peace between warmongers and sworn enemies,
    and are merciful to those who find themselves in extreme distress.
We rejoice and are glad that we too are counted in your number.
Amen.

Fourth Sunday before Advent

Deliver us, O God, from our preoccupation
  with money, wealth, and property.
Stop us from being enthralled by the so-called prophets
    who speak about inner peace, yet ignore the cause of the poor
    and your call for economic justice.
Set a fire in our hearts, as you did with the saints of old,
    that we may not place a burden, great or small, on anyone.
May we endure to the end and be saved.
Amen.

Third Sunday before Advent

O undefeated God, give us strong hearts as we wait
  in these days between slavery and the promised land.
Ever-attentive God, keep us watching, alert,
    and ready for the day of your coming.
May your wisdom be the mark of our lives
    that guides and determines the form and shape
    of the days that remain for us.
As we wait, take hold of our lives with a deep sense of urgency
    until justice is enjoyed by all nations
    and right living is central to our global culture.
Amen.

Second Sunday before Advent

As we get closer to your great day of coming,
    we are stilled, O Lord, in silence before you.
As we have declared over generations, you are our only refuge.
We have sought to follow you daily;
    teach us to apply our hearts continually to wisdom.
Come, destroy the works of evil apparent in the world about us
    and hidden deep within our hearts.
Come, destroy the injustice in our economy that gives extra
    to the rich and steals from the poor the little they possess.
As we wait for you to come,
    keep us mindful in these days that sometimes seem so dark.
Amen.

Christ the King

O Jesus Christ:
King, like no other monarch we have ever seen;
Ruler, who governs with fairness and compassion
    in a manner we have never known before;
Shepherd, who lays down his life for the sheep
    and brings them out from danger;
make us ready to receive you,
    for you are coming to see how we have:
    fed you in the hungry;
    offered you drink in the thirsty;
    welcomed you in the stranger;
    clothed you in the naked;
    cared for you in the sick;
    and visited you in the prisoner.
Come, O King, and rule in our hearts.
Amen.

Year B

The First Sunday of Advent

On this Advent day we cry,
    "How long, O Lord, before you come and deliver us?"
And you reply, "Be watchful, for I am coming to redeem you."
So we wait for you to come,
    with a waiting that often gives way to impatience.
Tear open the heavens and come down!
We are only clay; come and shape us
    that we may be ready to receive your promised newness.
Amen.

The Second Sunday of Advent

Unsettle us, Lord, with the stirring voice of John the Baptist.
Cause us to cry out in the wildernesses and barren places
    of life to demand a fair deal for all people.
Use us to bring down high mountains of injustice
    and lift up valleys full of broken, dispirited people.
Cause us to speak tenderness to the destitute
    and distressed and comfort to the excluded,
for your unstoppable ways are coming
    and nothing in heaven or earth will stop them.
Amen.

The Third Sunday of Advent

Heart-turning and fear-quenching God,
we dream of your radical ways
    and look forward to your control-defying freedom.
We hope and we wait and we weep.
Our mourning allows us to believe
    your audacious promise of return.
Keep us from smothering the fire of your Spirit,
    or despising your love of justice.
We wait and we watch, with love.
Amen.

The Fourth Sunday of Advent

Let it be to us, O God, as it was to Mary.
You have spoken and given grace
    in former times of emptiness and exile,
    so do it again in our day.
Let us be servants according to your will.
Let us also be bearers of the mystery
    carried by saints over many generations.
Be with us as you were with those in former times,
    as we, too, crave your presence.
Amen.

Christmas Eve

O Son of Mary,
as we celebrate this season,
help us to remember that we are light-bearers for all creation
    until you return to make all things new.
May we be as unthreatening to the poor and disadvantaged
    as a child lying in a manger,
but as subversive to the rich and powerful as a man hanging on a cross.
Amen.

Christmas Day

You have come among us: the only-begotten; the firstborn;
    the Word become flesh; born of Mary.
You have come to make all things new.
Light and Life, we greet you, born this happy morning.
You have come to where we are.
We have come to receive immeasurably more
    than we had ever dared to assume to ask.
Glory to God in the highest heavens!
Amen.

The First Sunday of Christmas

Carefully and wonderfully you made us in your image, Creator God,
  a chip off the ancient block.
Surprisingly and daringly, you sent Jesus to us
  in humanness and limitation.
Help us to receive the child of grace into our lives,
  that we too may say, "Abba, Dad"
  without awkwardness or embarrassment.
Keep us from retiring from our calling
  until all have known this great happening
  in the one born of Mary.
Amen.

The Second Sunday of Christmas

Incarnate God, in-dwelling life,
  reach into our brokenness and sorrow.
Find us in our lostness.
Answer us in our questioning.
Enliven us in our indifference.
We want to dance and sing and revel
  in all that has been lavished upon us.
We want our hope to be renewed and set free
  from our worlds of illusions and pipedreams,
    so that we may discover reality in the Word become flesh.
Make known your presence here today.
Amen.

The Epiphany

If magi, kings, and wise men are called, O God,
     then call us too.
If unbelievers who follow their fortunes in the stars are included,
      then include us too.
If spiritually dubious elders can be among the first to see your Son,
     then let us see him too.
We want light in our darkness and unbelievable visions to behold.
But do not just call us to follow:
     call the nations; call the excluded; call the bored and befuddled;
     and call those whose lives are rapidly passing them by.
Amen.

The Baptism of Christ
The First Sunday of Epiphany

You do not call us to christen nicely, Jesus of Nazareth;
     you call us to baptize into danger and subversiveness.
Through the waters of death you make us to pass,
     without knowing certainties beyond.
As John baptized into affirmation and conflict,
may we as your church not be coy about calling each
     to take up their cross into unknown futures.
You promised that if we lose our life for your sake,
     we will find it.
And so now, Lord, we take you at your word.
Amen.

The Second Sunday of Epiphany

We are here, Lord, for you have called us,
    and as we are here, speak, for we are listening.
You have searched us out from our darkened places,
    you know us more thoroughly than we know ourselves.
We have no bolthole to run to,
    no escape from your searching, no place to hide.
We are through with weeping and sighing:
    we want to see heaven opened up
    for the wonders that it holds,
    for honest and trustworthy relating,
    and for the coming of the Son of Man.
We are here, for you have called us,
    and as we are here, speak, for we are listening.
Amen.

The Third Sunday of Epiphany

Most High God, blesser of the ancient Abraham,
    may your peace be upon Israel,
    may your peace be upon Palestine,
    may your peace be upon Christians,
    may your peace be upon Muslims,
    may your peace be upon people
    of all creeds and orientations, colours and persuasions.
In Christ you transformed the old into the new,
    the ordinary into the special,
    and religious duty into loving faithfulness.
As in the despised towns of Galilee, come to where we are,
    with signs of hope for untouchables and touchables alike.
Amen.

The Fourth Sunday of Epiphany

Omnipotent God, we live in a world of conflicting powers;
   sometimes they make war with each other,
   sometimes they make war with us, your baptized people.
In Christ, you rattled these powers
   and disturbed their crooked tendencies.
In Christ, your light shone into their darkness,
   exposing what had not been seen before.
In Christ, your life-giving power
   undid the forces of ill-health and disease.
They knew who he was and could not fail to say,
and we now know who you are and must not fail to speak.
O Lord, rule all powers of evil with an iron rod and set humanity free.
Amen.

The Presentation of Christ in the Temple
Candlemas

O God, the young couple who came to you
   presenting a child that he might be "Holy to the Lord",
paid their fee and got more than they bargained for.
You presented to them two aged people,
   weathered of skin but wise of years;
one saw salvation and warned of great danger, sorrow, and hope,
the other saw redemption, joy, and a message to tell.
As we present to you our muddled hopes and conflicted desires,
make us ready to receive whatever you may give,
   be it joy or sorrow, consolation or turmoil.
Then we will journey in your kingdom, on your way,
   immersed in your love.
Amen.

Proper 1

All-pervading God, we feel like minute grasshoppers before you.
It seems from our perspective
    that you sit high above the circle of the earth,
    stretching out your greatness across the heavens.
When you ask: "Have you not known?", "Have you
    not heard?", we have to admit that we have.
You are power to the faint,
    strength to the powerless,
    and to those who wait . . .
    you cause them to rise up like soaring eagles,
    to run, and not become weary,
    to walk, and not faint.
We recognize that we have an obligation
    to voice such good news
    and communicate your radical freedom.
Amen.

Proper 2

O restorer and healer of unlikely people;
    lift us when we are hard-pressed,
    make whole our broken bodies, minds, and spirits,
    and bring us life when our resources are spent.
Come, turn our wailing into dancing,
    our grief into laughter,
    and our despondency into courage.
Though we may weep throughout the night-time hours,
    with you, joy accompanies the dawn.
O restorer and healer of unlikely people,
    do not overlook us today.
Amen.

Proper 3

We are a weary people, and even though we rarely voice it,
    we are often weary of you too.
Weary and exhausted. Lost and lonesome.
    Burdened and weighed down.
We chase empty promises and false rumours,
    looking for easy solutions to our well-voiced disappointments.
Embed us back into your faithfulness,
    your remembering of sins no more,
    your "Yes" and your "No",
    and your closeness to the needy and poor.
By so doing, bring to life that new thing
    you have promised from of old,
    today, in us, and in all people.
Amen.

The Second Sunday before Lent

God, from before all beginnings, from outside of space and time,
    from what cannot be understood or imagined;
in Jesus you are the image of invisible,
    unknowable, and unreachable being;
in Jesus you have come to live among us, as one of us,
    in limitation, vulnerability, and rejection.
May we embrace your life, ever present to us.
May we allow your shining to enlighten us.
May we become dwelling places of your presence.
In you all things hold together.
Never let us fall apart or away from you.
Amen.

The Sunday next before Lent

It is good and frightening for us to be with you, Lord.
You both comfort and terrify us.
The mighty light that burst brightly at the birth of creation
    shines into our inmost beings.
We are not sure how much of you we can handle.
But you will come and you will not remain silent.
So let us inherit, like those of old,
    a double portion of your Spirit.
Then, we will not let you go and we also will not remain silent.
Amen.

Ash Wednesday

Merciful God, we are marred by the madness of contemporary living
    and brought low by the strength of our rebellion.
We are tired and exhausted
    by resisting the brutal forces of egos taken too seriously:
    mine; ours; theirs; and of nations across the world.
Create clean hearts.
Renew right spirits.
Open closed minds.
We are ready to embark on your plan for fasting,
    as we loosen the chains of injustice
    and let the oppressed go free.
This is the day of salvation.
This is the acceptable hour.
Have mercy on us, according to your bond of love.
Amen.

The First Sunday of Lent

O God of deserted and wild terrains,
we know that if we do not enter the wilderness,
    you will surely allow hard and arid experiences
    to come to us.
Show us what can only be understood in fierce landscapes.
Expose the futility of our perceived goodness
    and patronizing acts of charity.
Keep us attentive to you and to our true selves,
    until we have been stripped of all that keeps us from you,
    from others, and from ourselves,
    during the usual routines of life outside the desert.
Amen.

The Second Sunday of Lent

Jesus, rejected by your own,
    having to call your own chief disciple "Satan",
    and crucified by the powerbrokers of Jerusalem;
you set your mind on what was loving, just, and redemptive.
We, on the other hand, have set our minds
    on the glittering prizes the world seductively lays before us.
O name-changer God,
    you who tie your people into a bond of love
    for fruitfulness and visions of new horizons,
teach us the habits of daily taking up crosses,
    of denying self-promoting impulses,
    of giving up promises of worldly rewards,
    for the sake of saving our lives.
Amen.

The Third Sunday of Lent

We, O Lord, live in a house of slavery and a culture of illusion.
We have turned your sacred world
   into a marketplace of thieves.
We have placed a price on everything and everyone;
   we have sold our very souls.
We have bowed down to crazy movements, corporate logos,
   passing fads and fashions,
   pledging our loyalty without even a word spoken.
Expose our so-called wisdom
   and the stupidity of our loudly-acclaimed economy;
take us back to your stumbling stone, your crucifixion governance,
   where none are robbed or overcharged or taken for a ride.
Only this will be acceptable when you come to judge this house.
Amen.

The Fourth Sunday of Lent

Lord, you endure, with your mercy, for ever and ever;
   but we need grace upon grace
   as we are hopeless at such enduring.
You gave your back to the smiters
   and did not shrink from shame,
   but we would often rather die than face any humiliation.
Only you can deliver us from our ruinous ways and rescue us
   from our utter foolishness, when we seek to build up, make strong,
   accumulate more, win success,
   and look robust in the eyes of others.
We love to dwell in such darkness,
   but your light has exposed the futility of our enterprises.
Come, Lord, and save us from ourselves.
Amen.

The Fifth Sunday of Lent
Passiontide begins

Covenant God, we do not fare well
   in following rules and commandments,
   so inscribe what is most important deep within our hearts.
Write it in our thinking.
Write it in our knowing.
Write it in our passions.
Write it in our instincts.
Then we will work and rest safe within your everlasting kindness,
   steadfast love, and covenantal faithfulness.
And we will see in Jesus the obedient sufferer,
   the compassionate forgiver, and the great over-comer,
   who died and triumphed for our sake and the sake of all creation.
Amen.

Palm Sunday

Broken trees and trampled coats
   welcomed the crowd-praised king.
While you rode in smallness on an awkward unused ass,
   the people began to shout
   their defiant enthronement hymns.
Today we welcome the rejected outsider dangerously into our world
   and frighteningly into our lives as he comes to judge and save.
Open the gates of right trading and dealings amongst the nations
   and rid our hearts of all that contaminates our praise.
Then people will say, "This is the Lord's doing."
Amen.

Maundy Thursday

You come to us in the simplicity of baked bread and fermented wine.
In the ordinariness of eating and drinking we take you,
    our Lord and Teacher, into our inmost being.
As we consume, as we feast upon what is broken
     and that which is outpoured, help us to be present to you,
    the presence we encounter in this sacrament of love.
Amen.

Good Friday

Bad Friday, yet Good Friday.
Held by nails, yet propelled by love.
Beyond human semblance, yet compassion embodied.
No form of majesty, yet king of all creation.
The one from whom many hid their faces,
    yet the one from whom we cannot take our eyes.
By our cruelty he was killed, yet by his stripes we are healed.
Thanks be to God!
Take us on the journey from aggressive assertiveness
    to courageous non-violence,
    from hatred to love;
for the sake of all people,
    in the name of the suffering servant.
Amen.

Easter Eve

We heard him cry, "It is finished!"
And we feel we are finished too, O Lord.
Baptized into his death.
Immersed in his forsakenness.
Applauded by no-one.
In this threshold space and liminal place,
    help us to acknowledge our powerlessness
    without any attendant terror.
We do not want to remain in the darkness of Saturday,
    for it is not a restful void.
But hold us until your work is done, and death is defeated in our lives.
Amen.

Easter Day

While in our hopeless, inconsolable crying and weeping and sobbing,
    you shock and surprise us, O God.
What was thought unbelievable is true.
What was considered impossible has happened.
What was feared to be the final death has been overcome.
No wall, no door, no fear, no barrier or boundary
    can imprison our Risen Lord.
So put to death our limited expectations of what love can achieve
and place at the centre of our lives
    the Spirit of your transformative rising.
Amen.

The Second Sunday of Easter

O Christ, your disciples heard, your disciples saw,
    your disciples touched, your disciples testified
    and we have received the witness.
Transform our lives with your resurrection economy,
    as you did for your first followers.
Lead us to be of one heart and soul and mind.
Teach us how to hold things in common.
Make us a community of your kingdom where joy is complete,
and we no longer deceive ourselves about our shortcomings.
Then, we will not lock the doors of our lives or hold at bay the stranger.
Amen.

The Third Sunday of Easter

O Author of Life, we wonder and we stare;
we are startled and disbelieving at the way you work among us.
A murderer you allow to go free
    while the Holy and Righteous One
    is murdered in the public, open place.
Come and stand among us as we cower
    behind the closed and locked doors of our lives.
Come and bring your peace that confounds our delicate sensibilities,
    and opens us up to courageous new worlds.
Come and make us witnesses, for we too, one day, will be like Jesus;
    we shall see him as he is.
Amen.

The Fourth Sunday of Easter

O raiser of the dead, lifter-up of the downtrodden,
    carer of the vulnerable, and lover of the over-looked,
you act with a power that makes little or no sense
    in our world of tactics and strategy-making.
Teach us the wisdom of laying down our lives
    in order that you may raise us up.
Keep us from being seasonal and part-time disciples
    whose love is conditional, fickle, and transient.
Let us love not only in word and speech
    but also in truth and action.
Then we will know your greater life-laying-down love.
Amen.

The Fifth Sunday of Easter

You, Lord, are the true vine of life.
At best, we are untrained branches
    not wanting to be pruned, cut, or trained.
We fear we are non-fruiting branches, resistant to your nourishment.
Do not cast us aside.
Assure us that when you prune our lives and cut us back,
    it is out of your deep and generous love for us.
Convince us that it would be a most unloving non-action
    if you did nothing to us.
And then, through hardship, grow your fruit in us,
    and even in suffering, cause your life to blossom.
Amen.

The Sixth Sunday of Easter

Astounding God,
you pour your life onto undeserving people and many of ill repute.
You chose us from dubious paths of living
    and from suspect moral purity.
Your love is larger than all universes:
    uncontainable, indefinable, and incomprehensible.
We will surrender our lives to you, not out of fear,
    but out of conscious, determined devotion.
We will sing new songs of hopeful liberation.
We will learn to love, not for private gain or personal advantage,
    but out of self-emptying generosity, for that is how you love.
Amen.

Ascension Day

Alleluia!
Heaven and earth have become one place, no longer two.
You live and move and love and breathe
    where we love and hate, care and wound,
    build and destroy, co-operate and compete.
God of our times, your home is with us
    and our home is eternally with you.
No longer is there a celestial other world
    from which we are barred or excluded.
Remove from us split spiritual world-views
    and our dualistic preferences.
Now everything is in you and you are in all things. Alleluia!
Amen.

The Seventh Sunday of Easter

Good God,
you who live amongst the chaos and violence of our heaving world,
    where we argue publicly over vested interests
    and privately obsess over inconsequential stupidities,
lead us out from walking in this counsel of utter wickedness.
Then we will delight in your coming,
our joy will be complete even in a hostile world,
and we will live contentedly
    in the aftermath of your death and resurrection,
    for you will not leave us comfortless, or without hope.
Amen.

Pentecost

O life-giving, life-disturbing Spirit,
you blow into our lives with little or no respect
    for our ordered patterns, protocols, or procedures.
We may resist and complain about your disruptive ways,
    yet we ache and groan inwardly for something different.
Come, transform our desire for improvement
    into radical transformation.
Come, transform our wishful thinking into dreams and visions.
Come, transform our wild hunches into justice-loving prophecy.
Then we will live in the fullness of life
    and recognize that all creation speaks of the glory of God.
Amen.

Trinity Sunday

O great Trinity of love, you are not complex or complicated,
    just way beyond our understanding.
You invite us to know you, not through wisdom or great learning,
    but by humble living and participation in your life.
You are the ground of our being,
you are the ground of all being: Creator; Transformer; and Sustainer.
Use us as a theatre of your grace to stage your drama
    of salvation and bring healing to your world.
Amen.

Proper 4

You are the God who lingers in run-down places
    when we have long forgotten your name.
You are the one who speaks wisdom to us
    even though we no longer pause to listen.
We are a delicate and fragile people made of the stuff of the earth,
yet who carry deep within us the treasure of your presence.
We are easily afflicted and perplexed by what we see,
fearful of persecution and susceptible to pain and brokenness.
Remind us of the inner life that can never be eradicated or expelled.
Show us how to live each day from this inexhaustible resource of life.
Amen.

Proper 5

O rejected Christ, whose people constantly choose
     other trophies to place at the centre of life,
give us the desire to put aside
     all that we have hitherto thought important,
     that we may seek the beauty of humility in all things.
May we cry out from of the depths of our experience
     to find in you the One who waits patiently for us.
Raise us from our deadness and decadence
     that our inner nature may be discovered once more.
Then, as family to you, we shall inhabit the will of the living God.
Amen.

Proper 6

You, Lord, see differently to us.
You do not take into account a person's appearance or stature.
You do not consider their skill and abilities or their athletic prowess.
You do not count achievements or awards.
You, Lord, see differently to us.
Teach us to walk by faith,
     not by how we see from our perverted human point of view.
We have to admit we look with fear
     and make judgements with our anxiety.
Urge us on in the love of Christ where panic and terror have no place.
Mature your life in us, that we may live still and steady lives.
Amen.

Proper 7

O God,
we are intimidated by the giants we live amongst,
    and perturbed by the storms of life that rage about us.
Many a time we feel you have left us defenceless
    and vulnerable to great evil.
Why have you not heard our cry?
Do you not care that we are perishing?
Rise up, O Lord, do not let evil and greed have the upper hand.
Let those who are so high and mighty,
    know that they too are mortal and flawed.
Come to our aid, as today is the day of salvation.
Amen.

Proper 8

O God,
we have seen mighty heroes fall from grace
and many institutions we once thought indestructible
    crumble and perish.
How the mighty are fallen!
Out of the depths we have called to you
    and now in silence we will wait.
You are our hope.
In Jesus, you endured poverty and humiliation
    in order that we may be rich in what only ultimately counts.
So touch us and we will be whole.
Visit us and we will be comforted.
Until you come we will wait,
    for you are our only hope.
Amen.

Proper 9

We have waited in silence on your loving-kindness
    and we have not been disappointed.
No longer do we need to boast
    of our achievements or accomplishments,
nor exaggerate and manipulate the truth
    so that we look swell in the eyes of others.
In you we have all we need.
This is sufficient and we will be content.
In vulnerability and brokenness
    your power is made perfect in us.
Therefore we will not fear or guard our reputations
    as we follow our Lord and Master, Jesus Christ.
Amen.

Proper 10

Way-out and beyond-us God,
we sometimes feel we have never known you.
Unknowable, incomprehensible, and unfathomable God;
    how did we ever get entangled with you?
Yet we cannot escape you
    or evade your all-pervasive presence.
All we have is first and foremost yours.
All we see about us is the creation of your imagination.
Even the little we think we know is yours and yours alone.
How could we ever glibly wander into your presence?
You make the first move,
    you are the first move of all that is, and is to be.
Amen.

Proper 11

We are tired and worn out by life, Lord.
As a conflicted and contentious people
 we have run down our resources for living
 and depleted our ability to love.
We have over-stretched and over-reached ourselves,
 working too long into the night hours.
We believed we were immortal and indestructible;
 we believed we were gods.
Relieve us of our arrogance;
 take us to quiet and deserted places
 where, unnoticed by others, we can rest and be renewed.
We behave as though we have no need
 of a shepherd or a mentor.
But Christ is our peace; only in him will we find fulfilment.
Amen.

Proper 12

God, we have judged you unfairly.
We have been harsh and found you lacking.
We have lived as if you do not exist,
 strived as if you never cared
 and feared as if you never loved.
We have never fathomed or imagined
 the extent of your great love
 that surpasses all the knowledge we think we possess.
Prize open the smallness of our minds
 and the banality of our little lives,
 for we do not wish to live as fools any longer.
Amen.

Proper 13

Teach us to grow up, Lord!
Teach us to grow up from the old ways
    of manipulation and coercion;
    trickery and deceit;
    control and craftiness.
You have not made us for this.
You have made us for humility and gentleness;
    patience and forbearing;
    deep peace and unity.
Prevent us from living an immature faith,
    where we come to you only for what we can take or receive.
Create in us a spirit space that is clean and infused with integrity.
Teach us to grow up. Do not cast us away from you.
Amen.

Proper 14

Death and slaughter dominate the many screens
    to which we are so fondly addicted.
Lord, deliver our world, hell-bent on its own destruction.
We cannot see truth
    because of the fog of falsehood that surrounds us.
We do not recognize your goodness
    through the thickness of evil we live amongst.
Feed us with your food, to relieve our aching hunger.
Give us your bread to sustain us for all the testing times ahead.
For our part, we will stop being economical with the truth,
    give up taking more than our share,
    work honestly, and speak to all with kindness.
In this we need your help.
Amen.

Proper 15

There are too many occasions, Lord,
when we have been amazed at our foolishness
and ashamed of the choices we have made.
We have ignored the wisdom of the humble
and listened to the madness of the arrogant.
But you have not turned aside from us.
Teach us to seek what you desire
and to search out your knowledge and understanding.
Feed us again with your living bread, that we may have life,
life that confronts our stupidity
and destroys the death we have so much loved
and embraced.
Amen.

Proper 16

O God, unique and beyond compare, there is none like you.
We cannot closely define you with our human-centred words
nor shape you out of the stuff of the earth.
When people ask, "What is your God like?"
we pause in silence before we dare start to answer.
O unique and unequalled God,
to walk just one day with you far outshines
the years we have invested in acquiring and achieving.
Prevent us from fighting our fellow human being
in order that we may be free to contend
with the powers that have marred and marked your world.
May we abide where you always abide, for there is life itself.
Amen.

Proper 17

O Loving God, you who draws us deep
    into your unconditional embrace,
teach us the lesson of wholesome intimacy with you,
    with each other, and with all creation.
For us, intimate relating often turns self-gratifying and toxic.
Then we are driven into isolation, separation, and loneliness.
Help us to become people who are both quick and slow:
    quick to listen, to wait, and to welcome the stranger,
    but slow to speak, to anger, and to make judgements.
May we live congruent lives
    where our inner thoughts match our outward actions.
Then we will not fear or withdraw
    from you, from each other, or from creation itself.
Amen.

Proper 18

Lord God, you do not rob the poor
    or show favouritism or partiality.
But we are a corrupt people.
We say it is the rich who oppress us,
    yet we want to become rich ourselves.
Keep us from becoming the evil we despise.
Instead, may we listen to the voice of the child,
    the destitute, the foreigner, and the outsider.
Then we will neither reap calamity nor dishonour the poor.
Our works will prove our faith.
Amen.

Proper 19

O voice of God,
we have to admit we speak too soon and talk too often.
We enjoy a mocking, scoffing word,
    and speak about things we do not understand or know.
The saying is true: the tongue is an uncontrollable member.
Teach us restraint and quietness
    until Wisdom has taught us her lessons
    through suffering and cross-bearing.
Then, on the other side of silence,
    we may have just one word to speak.
Amen.

Proper 20

O Great Life,
we want to be counted among the happy and the wise
    about whom Jesus spoke so tenderly.
But without you, we cannot do it.
Take from us bitter envy, self-ambition,
    cravings that lead to conflict, partiality, and vain hypocrisy.
Lead us into your better way,
    so that we willingly yield to others,
    submit lovingly to you,
    and act peaceably in all we do.
Show us how to trust your way of life
    where the greatest is the servant of all
    and the most worthy task is to welcome the lowliest person.
Amen.

Proper 21

If you had not been with us, Lord,
    the raging waters of life would have overwhelmed us.
Teach us to pray the prayer of faith
    in the midst of chaos and danger.
Keep us from becoming stumbling stones
    to small and tender people
    who might believe without our religious hang-ups.
Encourage us to take our stand
    against tendencies that monopolize or exclude,
    for you are the great includer.
Amen.

Proper 22

When life has turned to distress and disappointment,
    the voices of life around us shout, "Curse God and die!"
But we have invested our all in you, and have no other hope.
O God, stand up and support our cause,
    for it is said that you are mindful of the vulnerable.
For our part we will discover what it means
    to receive your kingdom as a child
and seek out your image
    in the shadows of our uncaring world.
Amen.

Proper 23

At times, the grinding reality of life
    has become a tiresome burden,
    and your hand, O God, heavy against us.
We have cried out to you from our forsakenness,
    but we have not heard you answer.
Yet we have a great high priest
    and we cling to our confession with grim determination,
    even through our night-hour's tears.
While the world tells us to "keep positive"
    in a desperate attempt to keep our fears at bay,
we will instead hold onto your word
    and the simple actions of serving people
    poorer than ourselves.
Amen.

Proper 24

O God, we have seasons when we find it hard to trust,
    then our questions and doubts
    are in danger of overwhelming us.
Remind us again
    that you are the foundation-builder of the universe
    and the source of all life and light and love.
May we pray as Jesus prayed, with cries and tears of passion.
Alter our aspirations and so prevent us
    from becoming lords and tyrants over others.
But we have to admit
    that we are not able to drink from the cup that you drank.
So teach us to truly serve,
    for this is why the Son of Man came.
Amen.

Proper 25

Jesus, Son of David, have mercy on us!
Jesus, Son of David, have mercy on us!
Jesus, Son of David, have mercy on us!
May this prayer of faith emerge in our hearts
    during the times of our disquiet and chaos.
In our world of cruel optimism,
    may your priestly presence help us to taste and see
    all that is truly good and wholesome,
    unframed by spin or glamour.
We speak too easily of what we do not understand
    and utter wisdom's truths
    whose depths we have not plumbed.
Let us only become humble, then we will hear your voice.
Amen.

All Saints' Day

1st November

O Champion of the Saints,
we remember and remind ourselves afresh today
    of all that you have done
    through the lives of women and men,
    and girls and boys of faith.
In Christ we are bound to those you sent before us.
In Christ we are bound to those you place alongside us,
    yet still we may not know.
In Christ we are bound to all you will send to follow us.
In the solidarity of faith and love,
    we thank God we are one in Jesus Christ our Lord.
Amen.

Fourth Sunday before Advent

Teach us, Lord, to listen,
    to listen carefully for your voice in all its forms and guises.
As we hear you great commandment recited,
      show us what it means to love
      with our heart, with our soul,
      with our mind, and with our strength.
We are prone either to act too quickly or never to act at all.
Teach us to listen to the voice of those who travel with us,
      the cry of all cruelly oppressed,
      and the groans of nature itself.
Then our way will be blameless.
Amen.

Third Sunday before Advent

God of all kindness, look with compassion
    on the anguish, pain, and distress of our troubled world.
We are a people desperately in need
    of a better way to live and trade.
Our destructive habits are a threat and danger to our planetary home.
We continue to behave
    as if Jesus had not declared
    that his kingdom of justice and peace had arrived.
We continue to look for scapegoats
    as if Jesus had not offered himself
    as the last and final offering.
Raise up bold and brave men and women
    who will speak of your different way.
Amen.

Second Sunday before Advent

News of your imminent return, O Christ,
    both excites and frightens us.
We desperately desire your deliverance
    from this life of pain and turmoil.
Come to us quickly and bring us hope and relief.
But we also fear what you will find when you come.
Come to us swiftly and put right our wrong and crooked lives,
    correct unjust practices, and stay the hand of violence.
Come to us, Lord Jesus Christ, for without you we are dead.
Amen.

Christ the King

O Human Christ,
divine upon the ancient throne, ruling,
    not with coercion, exploitation, or terror,
    but with the freedom a monarch only enjoys
    when there is nothing left to defend or fight for.
Your reign and government is good news
    to the poor and downtrodden,
peace to those who live in the danger of warzones,
hope to those whose lives are blighted by defeat,
and wholeness to all who struggle with illness and old age.
Bring heaven on earth by putting all wrongs right
    and by reconciling us to each other,
    to all creation, and to you, for all time.
Amen.

Year C

The First Sunday of Advent

O Advent God of our hopes and longings, come to us and save us.
As we continually slip into the violence of war,
as we deplete the resources of the world,
as many live lives of shame,
    knowing nothing of the divine image within,
    come, fulfil your promise;
    come, enact justice;
    come, raise the downtrodden,
that the life of the Son of Man may be known here,
    for all people, for all time.
Amen.

The Second Sunday of Advent

O God, the creator of wild people
    who speak dangerous words of prophecy,
we need to hear your risky messages once again.
In our decadence, we are disillusioned
    and clothed in sorrow, craving new garments to wear.
Our ways of living have imprisoned us.
Our ways of loving have diminished our souls.
Our ways of leading have sent many astray.
Can we endure your purifying love?
Yet still we covet your unpredictable presence afresh amongst us.
Amen.

The Third Sunday of Advent

Cause us to sing aloud and not fear, O God,
    for you are coming to bring us home.
You are near, in caring for the stranger,
        and by gently bidding your people to come to that peace
        that surpasses our best attempts at understanding.
Convert us thoroughly to compassion and justice
        so that we will not take more than our fair share,
        draw wages that cause others poverty,
        or leave succeeding generations
        with burdens of debt or toxicity.
Cause us to live lightly and freely.
Cause us to sing and dance, for all creation's waiting
        to behold a wonder so much better to see.
Amen.

The Fourth Sunday of Advent

O Mighty One,
we make our journey again, as in years gone by,
        to Bethlehem, the place of littleness,
        insignificance, and marginal people.
We call for you to come to us
        and remember your promise of mercy,
        to fill the hungry with delights of goodness,
        and scatter the proud and haughty.
Look favourably on all who cry.
Give light to those whose lives are haunted by darkness.
Do great things amongst us once again,
for we do not want to miss the prophet of the Most High God,
as he comes in humility and secrecy on this day and every day.
Amen.

Christmas Eve

We wait with bated breath for the child of Bethlehem,
  lowly and unknown,
    yet bearing the promise of newness for all creation.
O God, at this festal time, dissolve our romantic notions
  of limited and superficial peace.
Break open our hearts that we may receive and give
  out of an abundance beyond all known resources.
This season, this Christmas,
  make possible what we had till now thought impossible.
Amen.

Christmas Day

We welcome you among us,
you who have come from before all time
  and beyond all universes.
You are the Word for the world.
You are the Word for our lives.
You are the Word of creation, light-bearer, life-giver.
We give you thanks for choosing to come
  to our small planet hidden among the mighty stars,
  to take our frail and vulnerable humanity.
You enlighten all people.
You rebirth us to become children of the Most High.
You are present amongst us,
  in order that we may live eternally present to you.
Amen.

The First Sunday of Christmas

O giving God,
you who comes to us in great smallness
in the Bethlehem-born Christ-child,
teach us what it means to grow in stature and wisdom
more than in the achievements and accolades
so admired by the crowds we live amongst.
Help us to find truth
whilst immersed in the conflicts of family and community life,
where generational differences lead to misunderstandings
and even hostility.
We are all your children: named, loved, and held by you.
Amen.

The Second Sunday of Christmas

Lord God,
in Christ you are before all time, outside all time, and in all time.
Come into our restricted worlds
and expand our foreshortened horizons,
that we may see truth and beauty
beyond our treasured preferences
and ill-informed conclusions.
As a child, you grew into your humanity.
As a man, you trusted our humanity.
Lead us to the place where we may find confidence
to live fully as the people you created us to be,
in all our humanity.
Amen.

The Epiphany

O Source of all Life,
we confess that it is easier to create stereotypes
    of those who presented bizarre gifts to the Christ-child
    than to discover their part in your plan.
We confess that it is easier to cast these aliens in nativity costumes,
    than to embrace and accept their foreign strangeness.
We confess that it is easier to categorize and label those
    who do not fit into our tidy, organized worlds, than to accept
    and encounter the outsider trespassing on what we hold dear.
So come, disrupt our ordered lives with the odd,
    the peculiar, and the extraordinary,
    to blow away our narrowness of view.
Amen.

The Baptism of Christ
First Sunday of Epiphany

You baptize us and call us by name,
    not by race, nor by creed,
    not by ability, nor by awards,
    not by anything except by name.
You call us
    from following other lords and governors,
    from the seduction of constant acquisitions,
    and from the expectations of parents and peers.
You call us to a world as you would have it be, where receiving
    comes by giving, and living is the fruit of dying.
Baptize us afresh in your love, into your new way of living,
    abhorrent to this world but life to our souls.
Amen.

The Second Sunday of Epiphany

O voice of God,
we must not keep silent but speak on behalf
    of the forsaken, the desolate, and the wronged.
You have gifted us with variety and multiplicity
    for the common good, allotted by the Spirit of life.
Reveal yourself in us.
Reach out to others through us.
Remake this fragmented world with signs
    that point to heaven and earth made new.
By water and wind, by bread and wine,
    by love and compassion, come, save our world.
Amen.

The Third Sunday of Epiphany

Lord, we are done with grieving for our loss of success,
    loss of growth, and loss of adulation.
We are ready for joy; our carefully crafted divisions
    no longer count for anything anymore.
In you there is no Jew, no Greek, no European; no African, no Asian;
    no slave, no free; no male, no female;
    no class, no caste, no classification.
So rid us of our biased judgements.
Defeat our habitual patterns of labelling others.
Stop us from stereotyping and prejudging.
All we desire are the pure judgements of a loving impartial judge.
Amen.

The Fourth Sunday of Epiphany

O God, in whose love all things can happen:
    open gates shut on life; enact the impossible;
    bring down thrones; lift up the lowly.
Inscribe on our hearts patience, kindness, and joy.
Place within us your indelible love that faces all things
    and longs for unbelievable fulfilment.
As Christ is salvation for God's lost people
    and light to Gentile nations,
make us beacons of faith, hope, and love,
    in a world devoid of these three.
Amen.

The Presentation of Christ in the Temple
Candlemas

You warned us of his arrival, O God.
You told us he would come with judgement.
You said he would stand up for hired workers, penniless widows,
    fatherless children, and landless immigrants.
We did not guess, though, he would come in flesh and blood.
We did not entertain the thought he would come and suffer.
And we certainly did not think he would be carried
    on the arms of such young parents
    on the day of his presentation.
May we truly meet you, encounter your presence,
    and see your salvation.
Then we, too, can say, "Lord, now let your servants depart in peace."
Amen.

Proper 1

To you, O God, the angels cry: "Holy, holy, holy is the Lord of hosts,
    the whole earth is full of his glory."
Yet we are a wretched people of unclean lips
    before such an overwhelming vision.
But you, Lord, have driven away our guilt
    and blotted out the stains of our wretchedness.
Though we have heard without listening—Christ died.
Though we have looked without understanding—Christ was buried.
Though we have taken without receiving—Christ has risen.
You have made us what we are,
    no longer to be afraid of holiness or the deep love of rescue.
Amen.

Proper 2

O nurturing God, we want to be like sturdy trees,
    sending out roots into life-giving waters.
We do not want to waste our lives
    by fellowshipping with vain egomaniacs
    or cynical and arrogant types.
As Christ has been raised, so we want to be raised.
We do not want to go down with those
    who, with a mocking laugh, have consumed too much.
We want to stand in solidarity with the poor in spirit,
    with those who are hungry, and all who weep.
Help us to stand with you.
Amen.

Proper 3

It is hard to come close, O God,
    when we are dismayed, distressed, and angry.
It is impossible to take delight
    in the midst of jealousy and fretfulness.
But all such things eventually pass
    and burn out their self-destructive energy,
so now we choose to be still
    and wait patiently for your rescue and relief.
We have fallen down, but you will raise us up.
We have been dishonoured, but you will restore us once again.
We have collapsed in sorry weakness,
    but you will give us unexpected strength.
Now, we will not curse, we will not judge,
    we will not condemn; neither will we wither.
Amen.

The Second Sunday before Lent

We may be from the dust of the earth,
    but by God we know we are dearly beloved.
We may be made of the stuff of the ground,
    but we need not be ashamed.
We may be naked before you,
    but there is nothing you have not seen before.
However, our sins are stronger than we are,
    and our weaknesses lead us to believe we will perish.
You ask, "Where is your faith?"
Before you, though, we have to admit we are both afraid and amazed.
Leave us not alone, O Lord our God.
Amen.

The Sunday next before Lent

Our desire is to talk with you, O God,
but if the earth trembles when you are announced,
    then we will falter too.
Still, though, bring us to the mountain to pray,
    even though we are hard-hearted and perverse of spirit.
It is your faithfulness that convinces us to overcome our fear
    and listen to your quiet tones and thunderous voice.
We have such a hope that causes us not to lose heart.
So in boldness and terror we ask,
    bring us to your mountain to pray,
    that we may meet you in all your awesomeness.
Amen.

Ash Wednesday

We wish to be reconciled to you, our God,
because the dis-ease of separation
    is a burden we can no longer bear.
We want to enter into heartfelt conversations
    about all that has gone so wrong.
We will therefore go to the quiet place, the secret room,
    to pray, be still, and wait.
All the false treasures accumulated over years of striving
    and from the fruit of our busyness
    have not hidden the turmoil of our souls.
But in you, O Lord, our sorrowfulness becomes great rejoicing
    and our reduced standards from decadent living
    no longer pose us a threat.
So we will pray, be still, and wait.
Amen.

The First Sunday of Lent

Robust and rugged God,
who doggedly led countless people across wilderness plains
    to teach them the deep lessons of silence, stillness, and solitude,
    in the testing phases of life,
give us the strength to resist the temptations
    of exercising self-gratifying power,
    taking the easy route to greatness,
    or causing a spectacle to impress.
Keep us quiet, unoccupied, and alone,
until we have accepted what can only be received
    outside of the madness we fondly call "business as usual".
Amen.

The Second Sunday of Lent

Often, we are not willing to be mothered
    by your protective, defending love, O God.
Our search for personal glory is both our shame and downfall.
    You, though, lead us to seek your face.
    You stand for us as a protective shield.
    You are the great help to lost and wilful people.
But now we wait patiently,
    for our fears have overcome us
    and our anxieties become uncontainable.
Make sure we no longer seek controllable change,
    as we now crave a root-and-branch transformation
    for our blighted lives.
This, we admit, is all that will set us free.
Amen.

The Third Sunday of Lent

"Hey!" you call, O Prophetic Voice, to those of us wrung dry
    by the banality and drudgery of everyday living.
"Hey!" you shout, when we are desperately hungry
    for something radically different to live by.
"Hey!" you declare, when we have no resources left over
    to offer from our over-extended existences.
But now you have caught hold of our attention,
    we will eagerly search you out.
Now, we will abandon our predictable patterns of thinking.
Now, we will cling to you and not complain anymore.
Now, we are convinced your loving-kindness is better than life.
Amen.

The Fourth Sunday of Lent

You, Lord, are the friend of sinners
    and companion to those beyond the pale.
With you, happy people are forgiven people,
    for their disgrace is rolled away.
Unforgiving and unforgiven people are rarely quite so happy,
    for they carry their burdens ever before them.
In our stupidity we seek refuge and identity
    in the busy schedules and trophies of life,
    or by consuming glamorous goods
    and other seductive paraphernalia
    that draw us into addiction.
There is no better place, though, to take cover
    than within your great acceptance.
Receive us, forgive us, and remake us fully your children again.
Amen.

The Fifth Sunday of Lent
Passiontide begins

God of pain and passion,
    whose greatness is found in humility
    and whose power of love is displayed
    by hanging on wood to die,
we offer you, today, our woeful voice of praise.
As we worship, we have to confess
    that all we thought was once worthwhile
    is not so important now.
In its stead, restore in us the ability to dream new futures,
    to hope daring possibilities,
    and to discover unexpected delights.
Then we will sit with those at your feet
    and be sure the cost is worth the sacrifice.
Amen.

Palm Sunday

This is the day of subversive, symbolic drama.
Set as a king to claim his city,
    they sat their Lord upon his peace-horse
    and processed him into town.
Unlike the people of old,
    we sadly remain silent at your coming
    and do not announce your alternative regime.
Let our praises not be songs of empty declaration,
but hymns which declare, in the face of self-important people
    and conglomerates of power, that the silent man,
      riding through the joyful, peaceful riot of ordinary people,
    is the one blessed of God.
Amen.

Maundy Thursday

As a slave-king, O Christ, you are abhorrent
    to our sense of decency and decorum.
Your basic actions appal us
    and we feel belittled by your washing and drying,
    your wrong-stepping and confounding of us.
But be as insistent with us as you were with Peter,
    for our habitual patterns of behaving
    reveal the truth of our need to be self-serving
    rather than others-serving.
May we have confidence to believe that true power
    is to be found in lowliness, and grant us the courage to act
    in ways that wrong-foot people of power, position and privilege.
Amen.

Good Friday

O Jesus, suffering Lord,
we did not expect you to die.
We did not expect you to suffer.
We did not think it would end like this.
Strung up to perish between two criminals,
    you once again do the unexpected,
    even though you did forewarn us.
Take us into the mystery of your cross
    and into the great gift of your dying,
    that we may enact your new regime
    of forgiveness, justice, and restoration for all.
Amen.

Easter Eve

O God, the grave and the gate of death remind us of our mortality,
    that our days are few and often troubled.
In valleys of deep darkness we find in you our refuge.
Be to us a strong rock.
Keep us from becoming overwhelmed.
Do not allow the cares and curses of life to overcome us.
Let this light-denied day be our time of preparation.
And now we will wait, for waiting is all we have to offer.
Amen.

Easter Day

Death-defying, shame-surviving Lord,
who startled women looking for a stone-closed tomb,
    we had not hoped your hope,
      and so our man-made optimism was crushed by your death.
You proclaimed that in three days you'd rebuild your Temple.
When you said "Temple" we thought "building".
You proclaim that you will build your church.
When you say "church" we still think "building".
Startle us on this your resurrection day,
    that we may hope your hope
      and live as your transformative and life-giving people-church.
Amen.

The Second Sunday of Easter

O uncontainable God, O irrepressible Life, nothing can hold you,
    no-one can keep your tomb locked shut.
The old regime of death and oppression has been routed.
No longer do we need to live by the rules
    that have polluted humanity and torn our world apart.
Destroy in us all that would seduce us
    into old ways of living and relating.
Send us out and make us passionate for a new orientation
    that is biased towards forgiveness, generosity, and just dealing.
Amen.

The Third Sunday of Easter

Risen Lord, you are life to our souls
    and death to our well-entrenched ideas and opinions.
We live in a world of murderous threats,
    persecutions, and violence against minorities;
    we cannot claim to be innocent.
In our crises of fear we dare not ask, "Who are you?"
    as we doubt we could handle, or understand,
    any answer you may offer.
In place of our anxieties, bring your life alive in each of us.
Make your love our resurrection energy,
    and may your light in us be a beacon of hope for others.
Amen.

The Fourth Sunday of Easter

Through great love and great suffering, Lord,
    you have changed our world and transformed our lives.
Through the faithfulness and long-suffering of a few men and women
    you have brought such goodness and justice to a world in travail.
In the winter phases of life,
    help us to dedicate ourselves to your works
    and follow the calling of Christ.
Then we will know that nothing can snatch us from your presence
    and that we are forever eternally one with you.
Amen.

The Fifth Sunday of Easter

O time-waster God, who, in Jesus, spent too many days
    with those who were least important,
    most unworthy, and self-declared offenders;
come, disrupt our comfortable holinesses.
Stop us from using up our lives in self-consuming busyness,
    so that we may have time to sit
    with those we consider beyond the pale.
Then we will receive visions and dreams
    which will dismantle our cherished certainties
    and enable us to see the world and its people
    as you see it—as overflowing gift.
Amen.

The Sixth Sunday of Easter

O God of Peace,
   we are troubled and our hearts are much afraid.
We want to shout out, "Come over and help us,"
   but we have no-one to offer us courage.
We want to find the place of prayer,
      for we only look in the predictable places
      and not in what is outside or unusual to us.
However, you do not give or lead or teach as the world does.
So help us to look in different places,
      to other people, and for new movements,
      to encounter your fear-defying presence.
Then we will find your Spirit the place of peace within.
Amen.

Ascension Day

Before you left your apprentices of faith, Lord Jesus Christ,
   you spoke again of the kingdom of God.
Over the weeks of preparation for your ascension,
   you told how things would be in a world ordered by God.
At your moment of departure you said,
   "Stay and wait for the promise of the Father."
We are distracted, though, from the pursuit of the kingdom
   by our desire for success in our time.
Help us to listen and learn and stay and wait,
      that we too may be ready to receive power
      with joy as you are glorified.
Amen.

The Seventh Sunday of Easter

O God of prisons and other forsaken spaces,
we cry to you from our places of loneliness and desertion.
Come to us and save us as our faith in Christ
    is weakened by our experience of life and pain.
But you, the Spirit of God, speak to us
    before our words have left our lips,
    and you call, "Come".
To all who can hear, your word is "Come",
to all who are thirsty, your cry is "Come";
    for you are always coming to us daily,
    hour by hour and minute by minute.
So now we come to you.
Amen.

Pentecost

O Spirit of God, life-giving, death-destroying energy of the universe,
    we welcome you.
Keep us from attempting to control, manage, or coerce your life,
for you will go wherever you choose and do whatever you desire.
Convince us that we no longer need to go to special places,
    or receive from particular people or gurus
    to know the touch of your life.
You are God the uncontainable, inexhaustible, and unpredictable.
You are God the Holy Spirit.
Amen.

Trinity Sunday

You, God, are the relationship of Father, Son, and Holy Spirit,
    creator of our relational universe.
Isolation, loneliness, and exclusion are abhorrent to you.
Everyone and everything has a place
    in the world as you would have it be.
Convert us from our individualistic ways,
cause us to mirror the family resemblance by bearing the divine image,
and draw us into patterns of living that do not divide or separate.
Thank God, we are most ourselves
    when we are in relationship with others,
    with creation, and with you.
Amen.

Proper 4

We find it hard to believe, Lord, that you are to be found
    in the ordinary business of everyday events.
We find it hard to conceive that you can be known
    outside vast sacred buildings
    or other creations of human endeavour.
But may we find you in the stranger and the foreigner.
May we meet you in the singing of songs not yet penned
    and through the life-illuminating words
    of poets hidden amongst us.
Lead us into the simple way of life for the sake of hope, we pray.
Amen.

Proper 5

O Word of God, come to us.
Teach us not to be scared in your presence
    or intimidated by your intentions.
You give justice to the oppressed, you set prisoners free,
    you lift up the broken and bowed down,
    you sustain the widowed and the orphaned;
after all, you created the heavens and the earth.
Deliver us from the madness of believing
    that human rulers and large corporations can save us.
Prevent us from accepting the demented notion
    that war and its violence can bring
    any sort of redemption here on earth.
O Word of God, look favourably upon us,
    and be compassionate to your people once more.
Amen.

Proper 6

Lord God,
we see evil executed on a large and devastating scale.
Those who have, take even more.
Those with little, forfeit even the small amount they possess.
Hear their cry and give ear to our prayers.
Train our hearts that we may sense the pain of the poor
    and respond to their plight.
May we see how our riches blind us to your kingdom around us,
    the kingdom uniquely expressed in the unexpected,
    the rejected, and the outcast.
Amen.

Proper 7

At times we have become a defeated people,
    for the busyness of life has overcome us.
Our appetites have vanished and tears have been our only comfort.
In the loneliness of grief, the temptation to let our lives slip away
    and lose their hold on us has almost been too great.
We searched for you in the noise of life, but you were not there.
We looked for you amongst the crowds that surround us,
    but you were not there either.
So we sit in the emptiness of sheer silence, and wait for you to come;
    for we have no hope apart from you.
Amen.

Proper 8

To you, Lord God,
the source of all energy and life, we pray,
let us inherit a share of your Spirit as enjoyed by saints of old.
Place the wonder of your presence at the core of our being,
    that we may be compassionate and bold,
    gentle and courageous,
    forbearing and daring.
We do not want to follow the paths that crowds seek out
    or hanker after our own popularity.
We want to follow wherever you may take us,
    without opposing or rebuking
    except for the sake of the excluded and the marginalized.
Amen.

Proper 9

O God, the powerful and those who rule
    come to ask you to assist them in their mightiness,
    but all you ask is that they should be humbled.
You bring down great names from thrones,
    but tenderly lift up lowly, unpretentious people.
Therefore, we shall either fear you or be comforted.
Teach us to carry each other's burdens
    and cover one another's weaknesses.
Let us not grow weary of proclaiming to strangers,
    "The kingdom of God has come near!"
    by what we do and how we listen.
Amen.

Proper 10

We are tired out, Lord,
    and fatigued by the pain and angst of the world;
    no longer moved by the plight of others
    and numbed by the incessant reports
    of disaster, war, and injustice.
But your resources are inexhaustible.
Come, save all those cast aside by cruelty,
    defend those harshly judged and too easily condemned,
    rescue the desperate,
    and deliver the ill-treated and neglected.
Renew your voice of prophecy amongst us
that we may stand again alongside those abandoned by others.
Day by day, pray yourself in us,
    that we may be energized by your relentless love
    and moved by your tender compassion.
Amen.

Proper 11

God of all history, nearer and nearer draws the time
    when hostility will be routed and estrangement outlawed.
You will condemn both as lacking
    and we will be judged for participating in their corruption.
Teach us not to find our hope
    in mastering life and controlling others.
Our hope is in Christ, with Christ, and through Christ.
So train us to sit and be attentive to the only necessary thing,
    for this will not be taken from us.
Amen.

Proper 12

Lord, teach us to pray.
Take us into that inner place where we can sense you more clearly.
Deliver us from the noise of what we think we know;
    then we will meet Christ: fullness and deity embodied.
At the beginning of each day take us to a different starting point,
    that we may encounter the many wonders of ordinariness
    that can never be measured or numbered.
Amen.

Proper 13

We are a pre-occupied people:
    too much caught up in self-indulgence,
    seeking to disguise the discomfort of our existence.
You are the God deeply committed:
    unable to give us up;
    unable to give us over.
Redeem us from the so-called easy way of life.
Call us afresh to a re-ordered inconvenient life
    that renounces pious, romantic religion,
    and practises the memory of Jesus.
Amen.

Proper 14

Lord, have we become a burdensome noise to you?
We pray and chant and sing and worship with drama and colour,
    yet also while holding divisive spirits and self-preserving egos.
Lord, we have indulged ourselves with services and celebrations
    as if these are the purest form of worship.
Become an intrusive presence in our lives
    and do not remain silent anymore.
Mould us into people of your kingdom, ready and generous,
with a conviction that your way will one day finally fully come.
Amen.

Proper 15

O mighty, devastating God,
you come looking for justice,
    but all you see is bloodshed;
you come expecting righteousness,
    but all you hear is the weeping of victims.
It is no wonder you have come
    to tear down the idolatry we have made of our churches
    and the self-seeking agendas they serve.
Inspire us with the great crowd of saints who have gone before:
    women and men who never saw what was promised,
    but nonetheless daringly followed you in faith.
Call us beyond ourselves, and lead us into the suffering that heals.
Amen.

Proper 16

Before you, Lord, we are small and silent;
    we have no idea how to speak.
Long before our conception, we were known to you in love.
It is rare that we see each other with the eyes of love,
    yet you see us so intimately every day.
You are the one we can run to and hide in.
You are the one who will never shame us.
You are the one who cannot be shocked or shaken
    by our outrageous behaviour.
Come, set us free from the years of being bent double and lost.
Come, deliver us, O great, consuming God.
Amen.

Proper 17

We have not always welcomed your word gladly, O Lord.
    What we have touched, we have defiled.
    What we were told, we have forgotten.
We have traded glory for a basket full of junk.
We are sick and tired of all we have done.
But you are God the rescuer,
    who repeatedly brings your people
    out of slavery, deceit, and self-delusion.
Save us again from our love of money.
Keep us faithful to our closest bonds.
Do not let us take titles or positions of honour,
    for humility is in your blood.
Amen.

Proper 18

Attentive God,
eternally present to us and ever desirous of our communion,
    you long to see your image fully alive in us.
To you, we are not commodities to be expended
    or resources to be deployed.
We are not numbers in a cosmic inventory
    or figures on a balance sheet of life.
You do not count us, you love us.
You know us through and through.
In you we live and have our being; nothing is out of sight to you.
Keep us alive to your presence; we do not wish for a lesser purpose.
Amen.

Proper 19

What have we done to your world, O Great Creator God?
Our patterns of greed and consumption
    have failed a billion lives or more
    and ruined once abundant lands.
We thought we were so clever, living outside of your design.
We believed we were so mighty, assuming you were dead and gone.
Do not leave us to our own warped devices, for we shall surely die.
But search us out and carry us home to life and great rejoicing.
Amen.

Proper 20

Lord, when will you come and save your people?
Our joy has gone, our grief is debilitating,
    and a sickness has infected our spirit.
We are not distressed because our churches are no longer full.
We are not even so disturbed when others wilfully oppose us.
What we find too great to bear
    is when people simply choose to ignore you
    and discount our story as worthy of any consideration.
Lord, it is harder to be ignored than opposed.
We therefore pray for all in authority and those who wield power,
as you desire that all shall be saved.
Amen.

Proper 21

It is easy for us to become an embattled people, O God,
    as the powers of this world set themselves against our door
    with philosophies too hard for us to counter or disprove.
This period of our history is not helpful or accommodating
    to people of faith.
Show us what to say and what not to say.
Show us how to be content with little or with plenty.
We shall wait for you, O Lord, and be still.
Amen.

Proper 22

There is a loneliness in your church, O Lord.
Once we used to be great and significant,
and the people of the nation came to our doors
    for their liturgies of life.
But now the landscape has altered
    and it is hard to sing our hymns and songs
        when cynical or mocking ears are listening.
You know our faithfulness and you have seen our tears.
Increase our faith and keep from us the curse of timidity.
Amen.

Proper 23

We sometimes feel as if we have been left behind
    by many who have moved on to futures that are not ours.
In our culture of rushing on and leaving behind,
    teach us to stay and seek the welfare of others,
    and pray on their behalf.
Through the many trials and difficulties of the Fridays of life,
    raise us, we pray, to live as resurrection Sunday people,
that we may embody the peace of Christ,
    rejoice in the goodness of life about us,
    and live with thankful hearts.
Amen.

Proper 24

O God, you have etched on our hearts the antidote
    to ways that are corrupt and power-hungry.
Your Word has sustained us through thick and thin
    even though we have often looked elsewhere
    for nourishment and hope.
The pull of competitive and coercive practices is strong,
    and has tempted us away from you.
But we will stay with you and plead our case
    with the fine thread of faith that binds us to you.
Amen.

Proper 25

God, be merciful to us sinners.
We cannot easily stand and claim
    that we are better or purer than anyone else.
We are much reduced as people,
    having spent our lives in point-scoring and resentment.
Our sins are stronger than we are,
    but you will erase the record.
In your protest against piety,
    you pour down your torrents of goodness
    on those who stand far off in humility to pray.
Amen.

All Saints' Day
1st November

We walk with you in faith, O Lord:
    with those who have gone before us,
    with those who walk beside us,
    and with those who will one day follow after us.
Today we acknowledge our place amongst the great congregation,
    spanning the course of history
    and bridging the divisions between cultures.
Rip us free from our isolated and individualistic worlds,
    to see our part in the unbreakable chain
    of unnumbered faithful saints in heaven and on earth.
Amen.

Fourth Sunday before Advent

Come, Lord, set our hearts on fire for you.
Come, Lord, put away our taste for committing evil.
Come, Lord, convert us thoroughly and fully to you.
Our pretentious liturgies and endless songs of praise
    have become a burden to you
    when we do not fulfil your call for justice.
Bring salvation to this house today!
Change our anxiety-driven lives
    and our insatiable desire to have more.
Come, visit us afresh, for that is all we need.
Amen.

Third Sunday before Advent

Lord Jesus Christ,
we follow you faithfully, day by day,
    yet our hearts are weary and troubled
    by all we see happening around us.
We know you live today, never again to die or decline.
But are you for us or against us?
Hear us as we call upon you.
Listen to our cries.
Bend your ear low to us.
Answer our questions and petitions,
for you are a long time coming,
    and we fear we will not have the strength to hope and wait.
Restore the brokenness of our lives
    and bring your wholeness swiftly.
Amen.

Second Sunday before Advent

O freedom-granting God,
our lives are dominated by corporations and powers
    who determine the shape of our lives
    and take resources from the vulnerable.
You promised all such empires would be brought low,
    so come, judge with equity,
    and extricate us from our collusion with all who oppress.
We hear many bizarre and frightening voices
    from our contemporary false prophets
    who grace our media channels.
Keep us faithful to the true Messiah and prophet
    whose reappearing we await.
Amen.

Christ the King

Jesus, Lamb upon the throne,
    when we had expected a conquering hero;
Jesus, crowned with many thorns,
    when we had expected only jewels;
Jesus, forgiving King,
    a grace not seen before in ruling lords and masters;
come with your fresh design for us, founded before time began.
Wrong-foot us, once again, with new visions
    of how life can be nurtured,
    governance managed,
    and people liberated.
In Christ, God has become King;
    we will pause and be still before your unusual magnificence.
Amen.

Postscript

My experience of prayer

A little while ago I was asked by my local church if I would say something about my experience of prayer. It was not to be a sermon but rather a chance for me to tell the story of my prayer life and how it has worked out for me. Since my wife and I moved into the neighbourhood two years earlier I had not been asked to do anything at the church as I work most Sundays as a prison chaplain, so I felt honoured to be asked. Then, when I thought about it, I was a little unnerved. I realised it would be easier to preach on the topic, to speak about prayer in general terms rather than talk about *my* prayer life specifically; it felt too personal, too close to home. There are many things about my life that I want to keep private and prayer is one of them. In support of this I could quote the words of Jesus who said we must go into our private place to pray so that others do not know what we are up to (Matthew 6.6), and if we fast to make sure that no one else can tell (Matthew 6.18).

However, when I reflected on the matter a little further I had to own up to the fact that the main reason for my disquiet was that I felt a fraud. I am hopeless at praying. Who was I to talk about prayer? Being an ordained minister in the church does not magically make one a first class pray-er, just as being married does not automatically make one a first-class lover. So within just a few short hours, I travelled from being delighted to feeling quite apprehensive.

I am amongst august company, though. St Paul said that we do not know how to pray (Romans 8.26), clearly including himself among the "we". This was despite the fact that he had the benefit of meeting the risen Lord in an overwhelming experience on the road to Damascus, and that as an apostle of the church he saw dramatic healings and witnessed many coming to follow the Christ he proclaimed—yet still he said he was rubbish at praying. There is, then, some encouragement here.

Over the years I have heard a lot of talks on prayer and read numerous books on the topic. For instance, like many others, I was told about the acronym A.C.T.S., the lesson being that prayer should be made up of Adoration, Confession, Thanksgiving, and Supplication. This was interesting information which sounded good and correct, but it changed nothing for me. I just felt that I was not making the grade nor applying myself to the task as I should. Teachings on prayer usually made me feel guilty and further from God, not closer.

I met people who told me about their wonderful prayer lives, sometimes calling them "prayer ministries". Some claimed they would pray for three hours before breakfast each morning or that God would wake them up at night to make them intercede about this, that, or the other. They were vocal about living lives of busy excitement, constantly moving from one spiritual experience to another. I have to say that it was not too long before I simply did not believe what they said. After all, a truly humble, Christ-like person would not boast about such things.

Over 25 years ago, when I was a vicar in inner-city Birmingham, I attended a conference on worship. I went knowing that the state of prayer in my life was dire, to say the least. I shared this fact in one of the small group sessions; a group member said they thought I would get the answer before I went home. The main speaker was Sandy Millar, who used to be vicar of Holy Trinity Brompton—one of the largest Anglican churches in London (subsequently famous for the Alpha Course). He simply said what he did to pray. He told the conference that one day each week he made a packed lunch and drove out of the city for the best hours of the day for a weekly retreat out in the countryside. This, he said, kept his spirit alive. I thought, if he can do this while heading up one of the largest churches in the country, surely I can do the same.

This, then, became my weekly practice. I would drive out of Birmingham to a nature reserve with my sandwich box, some spiritual reading, and a prayer book or two. Did this make a marked difference to my life? No, not really—at least, not initially. In the early years I felt I was wasting time. There was so much work to be done back in the parish and here I was sat idly by the side of a lake. But I believed it was the right thing to do and the members of my family and church held me to it. So I stuck at it.

Over time I learnt two crucial lessons about prayer. First, prayer is not so much about saying words, making requests, or good feelings. Before anything else, prayer is about nurturing a relationship. It is about how I live with God and how God lives with me, in me, and through me. It is about finding how my life starts with God and ends with God. It is about me becoming fully alive as I, like you, am a chip off the old block, made in his image. Second, I learnt that prayer is about presence, about being there, about turning up. There is a saying which states we need to waste time with the people we love: eating, laughing, sighing, talking, crying, or simply being still, quiet, and silent.

In the garden of Gethsemane Jesus asked Peter, James, and John to pray with him, to keep watch. He did not give them a list of prayer requests, he simply asked them to be with him and keep watch—to be present and alert. But they failed three times. Again, I feel I am in good company. We need to waste time with God.

I am still trying to learn to be present in all that I do: to God, to my family, to the people I work amongst, to the person on the till at the petrol station, to life in general. It is an extremely hard lesson to learn, though. We all know we can spend some time with a friend or person in need, yet be somewhere else completely different in our heads, making a list of what we need from the shops or working out how to deal with a church member we have had an argument with. This is never truer than in prayer; my mind is always going anywhere rather than staying in the present moment. The result is that I demean and devalue the one I am with.

In the third Gospel there is the wonderful account of Mary and Martha having Jesus to tea at their house in Bethany (Luke 10.38-42). The text tells us that Mary sat at the feet of Jesus, completely attentive to what he was saying—she was fully present in the moment. Martha, though, was like a whirlwind in the kitchen getting the food and drinks ready for all, resentful and complaining that Mary was not helping. Then Jesus called Martha back to herself, "Martha, Martha". He went on to say, "You are worried and distracted by many things; there is need of only one thing. Mary has chosen the better part, which will not be taken away from her."

Being attentive and present is not the sum total of what prayer is, but it is the most important aspect of it. Without it we have nothing.

Do I ask God for things in prayer? Yes I do, but my expectation is that what will usually change is me, rather than God. Do I keep a checklist of prayers answered? No, I do not. My life of prayer with God is about nurturing the love between us, not about getting a result or trying to twist God's arm to do something. God will do what God will do, and my task is to humbly allow that to happen and then find my place within it.

I find it easier to pray with others—praying alone is a hard and sometimes lonely task. When I pray with others I find it best if there is plenty of silence, time for listening. As in another well-known phrase, we could say, "Pray at all times; use words if you must."

Sometimes I have found it helpful to carefully compose and write what I want to say. This book is the fruit of such times. By using carefully considered words and phrases I am better able to express my inner thoughts and feelings. There is time to reflect, change words, and alter nuances before committing myself to the prayer.

It is very rare that I get a letter through the post nowadays except a circular or invoice; so much communication happens electronically. A hand-written letter, though, is a very precious thing. Sometimes I choose to write a letter the old-fashioned way to someone who is dear to me and is going through an important or difficult time. A few carefully considered words can say so much. They nurture a relationship so much more effectively than a quickly composed and dispatched email. (Walter Brueggemann's collection of prayers has been a great inspiration to me in this regard.[1])

Not being a vicar now, I commute to work. I am surprised how the gentle twenty-five-minute drive across the countryside has become a valuable time for me to try to be present to God. During this time I either listen to solo piano music or simply make use of the silence. I never listen to the radio. As I travel in the morning it prepares me for the day; then the journey home resolves the issues of the day before God.

---

[1]   Edwin Searcy (ed.), *Awed to Heaven, Rooted in Earth: Prayers of Walter Brueggemann* (Fortress Press, 2003).

Throughout most days opportunities crop up to pray, as chaplain, with others. These prove to be the most moving part of my days. Prisoners who let you pray with them are often open, troubled, and desperate. What is important in these interactions is not so much the words of the prayer, but encouraging each of these men to be present to God who, of course, is always present to them.

Our day ends at home with a few well-known prayers and a simple reflection. My wife and I look back over the day to identify what has given us life and what has drained life from us, what we have been most grateful for and what we have been least grateful for. After a final prayer or two together, our day ends.

The prayers in this book will not solve anyone's problem with the struggle of prayer; such struggle is an important feature of any significant relationship. Instead, it is my hope that these prayers will help you negotiate the disruptive times of life and find God's compassion in all things. In this, I pray that you find how to be more present to God and to all reality than you were previously.

Also by Graham Turner

"For those who still live in 'empire', a book like this is extremely helpful and important. In fact, without this wisdom and frame, the Bible has often ended up being a tool of oppression instead of a gift for liberation."
— **Richard Rohr**

"An accessible, radical and rare example of the aliveness and relevance of both the Old and New Testaments. Allow your faith to be energised and made passionate by reflecting on the insights that are brought to you in this book."
— **Ann Morisy**

Available from
www.sacristy.co.uk